# Have We Had Easter Yet?

# Have We Had Easter Yet?

## Poems by Alison Pryde

*PETERLOO POETS*

First published in 1998
by Peterloo Poets
2 Kelly Gardens, Calstock, Cornwall PL18 9SA, U.K.

A catalogue record for this book is available
from the British Library

ISBN 1-871471-73 7

Printed in Great Britain by
Antony Rowe Ltd, Chippenham, Wilts.

## ACKNOWLEDGEMENTS:

"Have We Had Easter Yet?" won second prize in the 1994 Peterloo Poets Open Poetry Competition and was published in the 1994 Peterloo Competition poster/leaflet of prizewinning poems.

"Bull Fight" was commended in the 1996 Rhyme International Competition and published in *Orbis*.

"British Seaside, British Summer" was broadcast on Radio 4's *Pen to Paper* programme.

"Pandemonium in the Panel Room" appeared as a commended entry in *The Michael Bruce Anthology*, published by the Michael Bruce Memorial Trust.

"What I Would Like" was published in the Northern Arts Magazine *Keywords* and "You'll Sleep Your Wits Away" in its successor *Red Herring*.

"Waters of Youth" appeared in *The Newcastle Journal*.

"In Sister's Office" was published in *Poetry Digest*'s anthology of competition-winning love poems.

For Jo, Katie and Simon

# Contents

# Have We Had Easter Yet?

"Who are you?" asks my mother.
"If you're looking after me
I ought to know your name."

I show her me when I was small,
A faded photograph.
"That's Bobbins," she says instantly.

"I wonder where she is, she never comes to see me."
I go away. To get my mother's lunch.
"How good it looks. Please thank the cook."

Later I find it in the bin.
"I didn't know who'd cooked it,
So I had those custard creams."

She smiles at me with faded, muddled eyes
And says my name,
Then struggles off on shaky legs,

Looks for her stick,
Opens the outside door,
Calls home dead dogs.

## I'll See You Down the Lane

Clutching the ward's wall rail,
My mother's off to feed the bantams.
Where's the bucket? Do they need more grit?

"Come along, dear. Back to your chair."
"I have to feed the bantams."
They take her back and give her Ed the duck.

Ed's in bed, his cap on squint.
One wing is loose and dripping stuffing.
He has a knowing, cross-eyed look, often remarked on.

That night my mother has a fall,
Struggling out of bed
To go and shut the bantams up.

She breaks her thigh bone. Now she cannot
Walk, but moves her arms and other leg
Frondily, like something under water.

She worries: is the black hen laying out?
I tell her I will sort the bantams
And bring a needle in to sew up Ed.

"I'll see you down the lane," my mother says.

In the day room someone's crying
While she rocks a shabby tiger.
Caged in a corner, the parrot lady squawks.

## "You'll Sleep Your Wits Away"

My father often said that to my mother.
She dormoused into bed at half past nine
And slept till morning. In afternoons
When I was small, I curled into the space
Behind her in the high wing chair,
Dodging the backward thrust of knitting needle,
And egged her on to read to me
Till her head nodded and she fell asleep.

Now she is old. Her head nods on the pillow
Against the high wing of a different chair.
She sleeps and wakes confused,
Calls me her sister, asks for her mother,
Remembers far-off times when she was young,
Which happened yesterday,
And talks of knitting socks
For long-gone feet.

## Viola Odorata

"Come along, you youngsters, get in line,"
(Daddy was a military man). "Kiss Great Aunt Violet."
She was as ancient as the pyramids
And she had a funny smell. When we went to visit her,
Bouncing on the back seat of the car:
"Fusty, musty, dusty," we would chant,
"Here we go to see the smelly aunt."

When we leant towards her, bodies held
Stiffly back, barely touching our cheeks to hers,
We'd get a gust of the essence that was Violet.
Gin and lavender water, Daddy said.
In the process of the greeting / parting kiss,
We'd wriggle, squirm and weave to miss the hairs
That sprouted from a huge mole on her chin, dodge
The stale powder, caked in crêpey folds of skin.

One day, when we were living far away,
A letter came from her executor.
She had left us all her jewellery.
"For the dear girls, who used to visit me so sweetly."

Shame-faced, we opened faded leather cases
Full of amethysts, gleaming in brooches,
Bracelets, necklaces, tear-drop earrings that
Might have trembled — light lilac shimmer,
Set in silver filigree — from ears we only saw
Crammed with a hearing aid. Had she worn,
In the hollow of a smooth, young neck,
That huge, deep purple jewel on its thread of gold?

Opening the boxes, we were startled
By the smell: a lovely, fresh, sweet scent
Of violets.

# Pandemonium in the Panel Room

My grandfather's at his mahogany desk,
It's in the Panel Room. I have to pass him
To get into the garden. So I play
Grandfather's footsteps.

The smell of his cigar curls round his head.
I have new sandals on. They're Clark's. Blue leather.
And they squeak. The swivel chair spins round
And pins me down.

I shriek. My mother rushes in. The parrot in the corner
Screams abuse. "This child's an idiot," fumes Grandfather.
Grandma's pekineses, Ming and Ching, come bustling in,
Bark at the parrot.

"My God!" roars Grandfather, bounding to his feet.
The parrot makes its favourite noise:
Agonised yelp of trodden-on dog
And Grandfather explodes.

And in the turmoil, as the household surges,
I'm out, through the French windows,
Under the monkey puzzle, over the lawn,
To the pets' graveyard.

Shaken, I sink down on "NAP
1934 to 43", begin to suck my thumb,
Rock to and fro and dream
I am adopted.

# Boris

Boris was born under a wandering star
And, though they never tried to keep him in,
Gave him the freedom of a cat-flap,
He wasn't able to sustain a life
Of domesticity, but had to leave
For days or weeks of living on the wild side,
Under a gorse bush on the river bank,
Hunting for food. No one to ask. No one to thank.

Sometimes they'd go and sit there, by the river,
Call Boris and, bone-thin, with staring fur,
He'd come and rub and purr, but seldom suffer
Them to take him home again.

So they respected Boris and his way of life
And waited for the colder weather, when
He might come back, curl close to them at night,
Reverberating. But always away again,
Flash of pale ginger and cream stripes
Along the hedge, edging the corn field,
Back to the bank-side and the lonely gorse bush,
Under a wide and starry Autumn sky,
With a dog baying the moon across the river,
And maybe a rabbit for breakfast, by and by.

## What I Would Like

Sometimes I think I'd like to live alone
With just the dog, the cat, the donkeys
And my hundred best houseplants.
(I'd keep the neighbours, all of whom are sheep.)

What would I do?
I'd take the houseplants out for walks —
I'd have to have a rota,
A hundred is too many all at once.
The donkeys — they could settle in the kitchen
And sleep in baskets either side the fire.
I'd plant the dog and cat in pots
And hope one day to have a dog rose and some catmint.

And I would drink a bottle of hay
And watch wild geese go by.

That's what I'd like to do, I sometimes think.

# Dawn Chorus Line

As I walk out on a midwinter morning, hunched and hooded
In my old, brown anorak, belted with binder twine,
I have an attendance of birds.

Sparrows crowd and sway on twigs of hawthorn,
Chattering a hundred to the dozen.
Crows wait in the wings;
Jackdaws participate in dramatic domestic squabbles;
A squadron of yellowhammers, formation-flying,
Swoops in for a little-bit-of-bread-and-no-cheese.

Pigeons strut around the hen house,
Appearing and disappearing, like a small cast
Attempting the crowd scenes in Julius Caesar.
A brace of raucous pheasants rattles in.

Bantams scold and burble in their house,
Waiting for the raised shutter and their entrances,
One by one, high-stepping into the limelight,
Careful claws lifted to acknowledge the applause.

It's breakfast time. Half a mile away
A gun goes off. Someone's lying in a ditch somewhere,
Shooting at greylag geese as they sink down
To graze. Over the eastern hills,
The sky's splashed red behind the rising sun.

## Stars and Brambles

We sat in the summer garden
Till moths and stars came out.
Black dog Murphy pounced on one
As it wavered over the lawn
And sat with it between his paws,
Till the bright star faded, the frail moth died.

Charlie chatted of brambling
In the hot, dry lanes and of
Adventures in his quest for fruit.
Matt, soon to sail the Escapado
From the Virgins down to Rio,
Then to Cape Town or Madeira,
Talked of twenty thousand feet of sea
Beneath the deck and of steering by the stars.
Charlie claimed he was intrepid
In his passionate search for brambles.

Murphy bounded down to the orchard,
Throwing a challenge to the darkening countryside.
We left the summer garden
As the curved clipping of a sickle moon
Sailed overhead.

# Waters of Youth

When the windmill stopped turning, we had no water,
The tank was so small that we soon ran out,
But it's nearly always windy in Northumberland
And the sails of the windmill spun round through
Hot days and cold and the creaky old pump clanged and groaned.

The water bubbled up clear and fresh,
You could lift the lid over the well,
(If you were strong enough)
And smell it: pure, cold and sweet.

But when it ran into the farmhouse,
It was deep orange-brown and thick as gravy.
It dripped through a filter before we could drink it.
We weren't suntanned by the long, hot summers
Of childhood, we were stained brown
By the waters of youth.

And the old lead pipes became more and more blocked
Till the water forced its way through a hole
No wider than a needle, and the pressure dropped
To a trickle and the steading of cattle sucked up
The water before it could reach us.

Then the taps in the house would cough up
Blobs of bright rust and my mother would rush
To the door to complain and my father would say,
"That's her again, shouting all over the morning."

We're on the mains now, with new pipes.
The water is clean and flat, with no tang.
When you turn on the tap, though, it's usually there.

But when I hear water pattering, rattling,
Thudding into an empty container,
I am a child again, waiting by the tank in the farmyard,
To welcome the whisper of wind.

## Slow Sunday

We sat on the wall and watched her through the window,
watering the telephone. Well. It had been a dry summer.
She was wearing the cardigan with three sleeves
She'd knitted the time they'd left her two days
In Outpatients. She saw us watching her,
But she ignored us and sprinkled Baby Bio on the video,
Then, seizing the remote control, beamed up the cat.
"I wonder what she's on," mused Maurice.
"I'd really like some."

Gawain was throwing pebbles at a garden gnome,
Scored a straight hit on one throttling a goose.
We swung our legs against the wall and sucked up
Ice cream cones we'd nicked from Mr Frosty Top.
He was lying underneath his van,
Looking for a funny noise. Flavour of the month
Was pistachio and diesel.

Across the park a game of cricket
Was studded by loud roars of "Howzat?"
And the smack of leather upon willow
As another bored spectator kicked a tree.
Hand-crafted, wild duck wind chimes on the patio
Quacked softly in the evening breeze.

We jumped down off the wall
As the cracked church clock chimed clonk
Instead of boing, and trailed off home,
Through summer dusk, to get the dog
To eat our homework.

## Hospice Lax 1954

When you were ill at school
You told the housekeeper.
It was a nuisance.
You could tell by how she sighed.

Unless you were unconscious or delirious
You packed and walked the mile
(Well, half a mile) to the school hospice.
There you had a bath in disinfectant
And struggled into a tight-sheeted,
Hospital-cornered bed of aching coldness,
Longing for a "hottie" and for home.

And no matter what was wrong with you,
'Flu, twisted ankle, earache, d. and v.,
You knew, last thing at night,
There would be a little glass,
Brought in by Matron:
A long, long draught of vintage,
Senna, castor oil, syrupafigs,
It tasted like a mixture of all three,
Hospice laxative, to keep you regular,
Give you vile cramps
And guaranteed to get you up next day.

I think that's when
My irritable bowel syndrome started . . .

## The Lie

Before I told the lie the sun was shining
And my best friend had given me a sweet.
The windows of the classroom were wide open
And someone whistled outside in the street.

Before I told the lie we read a poem,
The words were rich and round, the colours bright,
Pearls and rubies trickled through the verses,
There were sparkling stars and silver moon and night.

Before I told the lie we all got new books,
Dark blue exercise, with labels for our names,
And in them we would write our favourite poems
And, after poetry, we'd all go out for games.

Before I told the lie I had a packed lunch
With tomato sandwiches and chocolate cake
And a lovely juicy peach to finish up with
And I'd share it with my best friend, by the lake.

And then I told the lie. I wasn't talking.
"No, Miss MacCavity, it wasn't me."
And she said, "No telling tales. Own up, the culprit,
Or I'll give you all detentions. Now, 3B,

Close your books and sit with your arms folded,
I'll give the sinner just one final chance."
But I couldn't say a word although I longed to,
And I got more than one accusing glance.

The sun went in. And she took back the new books.
"I'll see you after school," the teacher said.
She left the room. Then someone took my satchel
And whirled it round and round and round her head,

Then hurled it through the still wide-open window,
There was a crash, a cry, "Are you all right, sir?"
Miss MacCavity rushed in and said,"Who did that?"
And with one voice, the class said, "It was HER."

# The Fairy Gymmy

Some fiendish dress designer straight from hell
Dreamt up the fairy gymmy. Cunningly
Constructed to flatter not a single
Adolescent female shape, it ignored
The probability of a bust, sneered
At the possibility of a waist
And ended, with a cheerless droop, mid-thigh.
Under it were worn serge navy knickers
And knicker linings. In the austere
Early fifties, the fairy gymmy
Was made of sort of colourless curtain lining,
Flimsy and limp, inclined to rot under the arms.
It had a dusty, stale sweat smell.
It was seldom washed. Boarding school had then
A cavalier approach to laundry,
But that's another poem altogether.

The fairy gymmy led a dark and secret life
In a school locker, coming out
("I'm a fairy gymmy!") for indoor games
And modern dance ("Be seagulls, girls! Swoop to the music!")
And gymnastics with Miss Andrews.
Of all the minor horrors ever I've endured
Gym with Andy takes the biscuit.
Menstruation, when you were permitted
To be "off", was welcomed with the sort of
Keen relief experienced in later but still
Pre-pill days, when you found that you weren't pregnant.

Three times a week we'd pound from locker room to gym,
A herd of heifers, charging the freezing corridors
Of a northerly Pamplona, heads down, eyes wild,
(Lateness punishable by extra gym)
Barely clad in fairy gymmies, galloping
Headlong and desperate, to fifty minutes
Gym with Andy.

## The Hairymen

Every Monday afternoon they come marching through the gate
And twenty girls are ready, for the Hairymen won't wait.
Half the house's hair gets washed today, the rest next week;
The Hairymen will pummel skulls until their owners squeak.
The water's always tepid, the bathroom chills and numbs,
The shampoo smells like sheep dip; they say it comes in drums.
Quick scrub, quick rinse, the Hairymen are poised for you —
                                    and you,
So shut your eyes, my darlings, when they reach for the shampoo.

No "Are you ready for Christmas yet?" or "Have you been away?"
The Hairymen have work to do and they can't be here all day.
Big Hairyman is gentler, little Hairyman is rough,
And your hair washed once a fortnight both say is quite enough.
So forget about a hairstyle, you know you'll look a wreck,
And lean forward to the basin as the drips roll down your neck.
Your eyes will sting, your ears fill up, your scalp will soon
                                    be glowing,
So grit your teeth — and shut your mouth — when the
                                    Hairymen get going.

It's wash and go, no mousse, no blow, no heated brush, no drier,
Shivering, we singe our hair before the schoolroom fire,
Then Matron chivvies shirkers out (she wears a wig, the witch)
For bracing hockey or lacrosse, on a freezing, wind-swept pitch.
It's better than a drier, the North wind through your hair,
Never mind the earache, it's wonderfully clear air!
So forget about pneumonia, bronchial tubes awash with phlegm,
Show gratitude, my darlings, and thank the Hairymen.

## Backs

It was all done in House Order at the beginning of each term:
Head of House first
And then a line of lounging, grousing girls along the corridor,
Ending with the lowest Lower Fifth, who fagged
For the Head of House and had a Grand Pash on her.
(Don't ask. Another poem perhaps.)
We all wore dressing gowns and looked depressed.

In the Housekeeper's sitting room, pens poised over
Their lists, the panel waited:
Dubs, the Housemistress,
Leila B. Brown, Housekeeper,
Miss Andrews, Head of Games,
And Daddy Mac, School Doctor.

One at a time we entered,
Took off the dressing gown, kicked off the slippers,
Stood naked, save for navy knickers,
Turned sideways one way, sideways the other,
Deeply embarrassed by the behaviour
Of unfettered, fairly recent breasts,
Which bobbed or bounced, were far too large
Or far too small. Faced front and touched our toes,
Then presented back view to the panel.

"All right, thank you. Next!"
We shuffled past the next one coming in,
Hastily tying dressing gown cord,
Pushing feet hurriedly into slippers.
Next day our fate was on the notice board:
"Extra gym: 8.15 am to 8.45 am"
Two, three, four, even five times every week for a whole term,
To cure: curved spine, round shoulders,
Flat feet, or (and this really rankled)
A crooked shoulder, which meant they thought
That one was higher than the other.

So you spent a term of extra gym
Hanging by one arm from a wall bar
And then, next term, they'd get you
Because now THE OTHER SHOULDER
Was the crooked one.

Backs. Appointment with hell
And Daddy Mac, Leila, Dubs and Andy.
But now my back is straight,
My shoulders even,
My feet well-arched.
But I think my legs are bandy.

## Hats Into the Firth

"Hills of the North rejoice!"
Was the hymn for the end of term,
And the loudest voices came
From the ones who would not return,
Who were leaving school for good —
Or ill, anyway for ever.

As the southbound school train rattled
Onto the Forth Rail Bridge
Carriage windows opened down its length.
Girls, delighted with their daring,
Leaned out, expectantly.
A minor infringement of a petty rule
("Overcoats will not be worn without a hat")
Was now, for the few, the happy few,
No more a punishable offence.

All the leavers' hats flew out,
Were whirled away by the wild wind
That screamed among the great iron girders.
Tiny, brown felt parachutes (house colours
Round the crown) suspending four or five long teenage years,
Floated, scattered, plunged, spun,
Rode the busy thermals for a space,
Sank down quietly or drifted out of sight
Above the steely, sculptured surface of the Firth of Forth.

Before the first hat reached the water,
The train had gone.
"Shout as ye journey home!"
And journey on.

## Scope for Imagination

This is my week for being Pollyanna
Of Green Gables, dressed in the cast-off frocks
And vile, striped socks Marilla and Miss Harrington
Retrieved from the Ladies' Aid box.
I'm growing pigtails, dyeing my hair red,
Snuggling under the warm quilt on my little bed,
Wearing skimpy gingham, playing the "Glad Game",
Driving friends and family insane.

Last week I was Jo March.
I said outrageous things, fell through thin ice
And only to sister Beth was I at all nice.
I wore a woolly hat when I wrote verse.
No handsome Laurie came my way, worse
Luck, Godammit, only bits of Fritz
In fractured German: "Ach so, Fraulein."

I've had a bookful of these heroines.
Should someone put that shade of shocking
Blood-red lipstick in my Christmas stocking,
There'll be no stopping me, you'll see.
It's Cruella de Vil and the Wicked White Witch
Of the West for me.

## Cat's Cradle

In a man-sized paper-hanky box, on top of my desk
Sleeps the cat. Too big for the box (it's not cat-sized)
He bulges over the edges and leans on
Roget's *Thesaurus*, the *Life and Works of Mozart*,
(I haven't read it yet but I will)
*No Fond Return of Love* by Barbara Pym
And the *AA Book of British Birds*.

Because I can't read any of them
Without disturbing the cat
I immediately want to read them all.

He knows this.
He opens one forbidding eye
And the tip of his tail gives tiny twitches.

This cat's not for moving.
He lolls against Margaret Forster's
*Elizabeth Barrett Browning*
(Which I forgot to mention earlier
Because the spine is turned the other way)
And, one eye closed,
Dreams, perhaps, of swallows, sparrows, mice,
The butterfly he teased to death this morning.

I really want to go to bed
With Barbara Pym.
"Tough," says the cat. "Try
Something else. *Success with House Plants*.
*How to Publish your Poetry*. That could be useful.
Agatha Christie's *Cat Among the Pigeons*, ha ha."

Yes, I know the cat doesn't talk.
I know I'm once again
Prancing down the primrose path of whimsy.
He may not talk, that cat.
I can sense, though, his contempt.

# *Wearing Her Pearls*

When she was twenty one,
In 1931, her father handed her
A jeweller's case, red leather, tooled in gold.
Inside, a string of pearls lay on cream velvet.

He never said a word.
He hadn't spoken to her for a year.
Used to his whims and sulks,
She accepted his decision to ignore her
And did not try to talk to him.
She never wore the pearls.

The crime she had committed was as follows:
She wanted to get married
To the brother of the man who was marrying her sister.

Finally, on her sister's wedding day,
Their father spoke to his second daughter
Just two sentences:
"If you're set on him, you'd better marry.
I'll never like the fella."

So, a year later,
My mother wore an oyster satin dress
(Her huge bouquet of rosebuds
Was the exact same shade of creamy pink)
And flat, lace veil, banded with August flowers.
My father beams beside her in the photograph.

The oyster satin train swirls,
A perfect shell, about her feet.
Above the demure neckline of the dress,
She wears her pearls.

## Coated in Creosote

We shot the rooks that took the winter wheat
And, when more came, all unafraid of scarecrows,
We devised a way to scare rooks.

We spread the dead ones out, in the wheat field,
And laid them on their backs, wings wide.
But foxes came and took them.

We shot more rooks,
Soaked them in diesel,
Spread them out again.

But foxes apparently enjoy
Rooks in an oily dressing.

Then someone thought of creosote.
We painted the dead rooks with it
And once more spread them out.

It worked.
The foxes steered well-clear.

And, seeing the stiff, spread corpses
Lying among the green and growing wheat,
No rooks came down,
But stayed in high trees, swaying,
Cawing, beaks lifted to the sky.

## Bringing Bad News

He twisted a tea-towel between trembling fingers.
"I'm glad the hospital didn't phone here first.
Can we go and see her now?"

He shuffled off to get his cap,
Leaving the heat on
Underneath the chip pan.

The smell of oil and loneliness
Hung heavily over the small kitchen.
"I never thought she'd go before me."

They left the little, silent figures
Dancing on the television screen.
Something to come back to.

## Bull Fight

Two enemies stood glaring head to head
Across the flimsy frontier of a fence.
Their small eyes glowed malevolently red

And then they backed, stamped, charged, and fields away
We heard the snap and crack of wooden posts,
The thud of heads, the roars that split the day.

Tails flying high, cows frisked about the edge,
Camp followers, they skirmished round the bulls
Whose blood spattered the air and streaked the hedge.

An armed force went to separate the foes.
The Charolais won the day. The field was his.
He bellowed triumph, took up a victor's pose.

The old black bull was led back to a byre,
Head swinging low, blood on his dewlap
From the stinging banderillas of barbed wire.

We patched the fence, cleared up the snap and splinter,
Bedded each bull, with cows, in his own courting,
Comfortably settled for the long, dark winter.

Star-struck dusk and frost-filled dawn now ring
With roars that threaten action in the spring.

## The Death of Pinny

When he was a little lad, he lost his leg,
Run over by the milk float.
They gave him a wooden leg, pin leg,
Then everybody called him Pinny.

"Let us play then," he said one day when he was ten,
To the leader of the street gang.
"Why aye, Pin man."
Pinny's hobnailed boot and wooden leg
Clattered and thumped towards them hopefully.
"Let's we have a game of cricket.
You stand there, bonny lad, and be the wicket."

Their laughter followed Pinny down the street.
Dot and carry one, away he went,
Making heavy weather of it.
While he was growing, his wooden leg was always just too long
Or just too short.
The hospital did its best though.

In the land of static gantries, frozen cranes
And smokeless furnace chimneys,
What work for a young lad with a peg leg?

Pinny took to crime
And became the noisiest burglar in the land.
His speciality was shops at night. In the flats above,
People in bed heard Pinny, crash, bang, thump.
They pulled the blankets up over their ears.
"He'll not come up here.
And insurance buggers can well settle it.
Good luck, Pinny lad."

And then a rash of similar crime broke out.
Pinny was appalled.
They were taking the goods and taking his good name too,
Careless lads, who slashed and bashed and left a mess.
Pinny took early retirement, turned gamekeeper
And night watchman.

One day they found his body
Round the back of Mario's chippy.
Head stove in.
"Where's the weapon?" asked the constable.
Nearby, in a dustbin, was Pinny's bloodstained wooden leg.

"He always said that leg'd be the death of him.".

## In Sister's Office, With a Tray of Tea

Leaving him for tests, more tests,
I drive home from the hospital
And, as I open the front door,
The phone rings. "We find he doesn't need to stay."

I drive the sixty miles back down the road
Through thundery August rain.
I'm shown into an office. There's a tray of tea.
"The doctor's on her way. She wants to talk to you
About your husband." He's there, in Sister's custody,
Grey-faced and shell-shocked.

Before the young, white-coated doctor passes sentence,
She gently takes away, puts down my cup of tea.
Six months. Perhaps. The pain can be controlled.
And then her bleeper goes. She wishes us good luck.

We look at one another. This is a play
For which we have not learnt the lines,
And there is no one here to prompt us.
Finally I say, "Shall we go home?"

Outside the hospital, things look just the same.
It's still raining. The car ploughs through puddles,
The windscreen streams with tears.
"Grow old along with me!
The best is yet to be."
Well, not for us.

## Country Funeral

Black-coated mourners, still as headstones,
Stand among the graves. Eight hold
The coffin's cords, wait for the minister's word.
His cassock flutters in the February wind,
Thin wind. Slabs of caked earth, green-iced,
Wait to be fitted back into the ground.

The little graveyard's cradled among hills.
In a field across the rutted lane
An old red bull leans on the fence,
Watching, blowing down his nose,
Then turns for his hemmel and the hay.

Snowdrops are out. Spring's coming,
But first some bitter weeks of winter.

## The Day the Men Came

I let him go out to play that day,
Though he was not quite two.
But ours is a friendly village,
We all look out for one another.

He was wearing his first proper shoes,
Full of innocent pleasure
He stomped out to show the others.
They were trying to catch turtle doves,
There in the square, beside the covered well.
I could see them from the window.
I was watching when the men came.

If it had been a gang from town:
Drunk, roaring lads, hell-bent on hideous fun,
Or careless, cruel kids, not understanding
How far too far was —

But this was all official,
Disciplined soldiers, obeying a command.
They had a list.
I suppose they got it from the census.
No one ever told us why they did it.

I'll never forget that day; how could I?
It was the time just after
The sparkle from that bright star died away
Over the village, down the valley.

## New World

Leaving behind
High tides of people, flooding over Europe,
Coming to
New Zealand, where unpolluted waters
Wash onto empty beaches,
Crash against vast, volcanic rocks,
And watching, far away on the horizon,
A yacht's white sail
Waltzing with the wind
On the edge of a sunlit sea.

# New Zealand Decorations

*I'm dreaming of a white Christmas*
Drones the piped music in the Christchurch stores.
Tinsel, sleigh bells, artificial holly
Hang from fake fir trees. The thermometer soars.

Out in the bush the rata's in full blossom,
Wild lupins lift like candles to the sky.
Cottonwool balls of cloud cling to the hilltops,
The bellbird's chiming merrily on high.

Cascades of waterfalls stream down the mountains,
Gleaming silver ribbons twist, loop, meet,
Water chains to decorate New Zealand,
The islands shimmer in December heat.

## West Side Story

We drive into Greymouth,
West coast of New Zealand,
On a grey, wet December day. Late spring.

Back of the town,
Creeks full of water bubble down the hills
And down the mountain creeps the bush.

At the junction of the Wap-waps
And McDreary road, a rusty and abandoned bus
Had been bound for Puckaroo.

The sign above the baker's offers
"'resh brea." Next door "Ladies fash" displays
Dresses a la Mode.

A young Maori lolls in the doorway
Of the "Zanadu unisex salon
sorry were closed."

Empty houses flaking paint
Are losing their grip on the hillside
And towards them creeps the bush.

When it has smothered
The psoriasis-stricken bungalows,
Will it crawl on, a land-based Kraken,

And swallow up Ladies fash and the unisex salon,
The Maori and the battered bus?

# The Boneless Groper

Is it some useless lurker in the park,
Waiting to worry women, after dark?

Is it the adjunct to a specialist's skill,
Examination probe or surgeon's drill?

Is it some Tolkien fancy, Gollum-bound,
Hassling little hobbits underground?

      No.
Caught in the waters close by Milton Sound,
Costing two dollars for a good half pound,
Grilled, baked or buttered in a lordly dish,
The boneless groper's a New Zealand fish.

## Auckland Aquarium

Once lordly ones of the South Seas,
The swordfish fly the tanks.
The huge fish loom and twist and curl
Away into the darkness.
The people stand on moving walkways,
Opening and shutting their mouths.

The pregnant female sting-ray
Is a source of much attraction to the males.
They cling so tightly to her broad, black wings
That frequently the water's streaked with blood.
Once she's laid her eggs, they're there,
Fighting to fertilise,
To get their rocks off.

Kenspeckle is the sea horse;
The sea mare lays her eggs on him,
The male gives birth
To a hundred or more sea foals.
As bat to air, chameleon to land,
So is the seahorse to his element;
Kenspeckle creature.

## Sonnet in the Words of Shakespeare

Now entertain conjecture of a time
In a New Zealand spring. No rough winds shake
The darling buds of May or violets dim.
The isle is full of birdsong and sweet airs
And sunlight sparkles on the southern seas,
Smooth waters for the shallow bauble boats.
And I, like Patience on a monument,
Smiling at grief, sit on a bank whereon
The wild thyme blows and where the bee sucks,
Here, in a lemon grove in Arcady.
Men close their doors against a setting sun
And finished now are all my dancing days.
I'll leave this garden, larded with sweet flowers,
And girdle half the earth in twenty hours.

## Bridal Path

The worst time of the year
For such a long journey; early November snow
And the horses straining through the drifts.
From the frontier, royal guards escorted them.
They reached their destination ten days late.

She was sixteen and had never seen the sea.
In the darkness the waves crashed.
Then lights and a fire to roast an ox
In the castle hall
And the chattering died away.

She clutched her fur cloak round her.
Two men rose from chairs by a map-strewn table
Near the fire and came towards her.
"Oh God," she prayed, "Let it be him,
The young one with the golden hair."

When they reached her, he stood back,
The young one. "God give you joy, brother."
The one with the grizzled beard, the sword-ripped cheek,
The piercing eyes that hardly saw her,
Took and kissed her hand.

"Welcome to Elsinore, my Lady Gertrude."

# The Friar Got There With the Letter

Now middle-aged and bored, so bored,
Nearly a grandfather,
(They'd called their first son Tybalt,
The second, Lawrence)
Romeo rarely remembered the scent of Juliet's hair,
The jasmine on the balcony.

His father-in-law had never quite come round
To suffering a Montague,
And Lady Capulet was a proper bitch.
Juliet was getting like her mother
And ruled her household with a rod of iron.
As for that nurse, one day he'd swing for her,
All innuendo and sly sexual digs
And, God, that laugh.

And Romeo still mourned
The quick-fire-silver of Mercutio
And pined for Rosaline,
His one, true love.

## "Kill Me Tomorrow . . .

Let me live tonight."
And morning came, and, as so often happens,
Things looked better.

Emilia explained about the handkerchief.
Cassio's leg improved, although he always limped,
Never trusted his own judgement and gave up alcohol.
Nobody remembered Roderigo.

They put Iago in a cage
And swung it from the battlements.
A placard proclaimed:
"Here, see a hellish villain."

Desdemona and Othello stayed together,
Though things were never quite the same.
"She has deceived her father and may thee,"
Rang in Othello's ears all down the years.
He stayed a prey to insecurity.

Desdemona's iron self-control
Entailed a sacrifice
Of spontaneity. Wary now,
And never quite at ease,
She watched her husband's moods.

Embittered Emilia
Never mourned the caged and swinging skeleton.

Iago won.
He poisoned all their lives.

## "*That Shylock presently become a Christian*"

He found it difficult to worship
Without something on his head.
He wore a shovel hat
But had to take it off in church.

He missed his skull-cap
And sparring with old Tubal,
The chanting in the synagogue.
Leah of the turquoise
Might have understood he had no choice.
He never saw his daughter Jessica.
He felt his mind and body
Stiffen into loneliness and age.

His days were empty;
No more bargaining on the Rialto.
The Christians roared with laughter
When they saw the hat's brim
Peeping timidly round corners.

The Jews spat at him.

# On Trying to Find "Happy" Poems

Poets are a gloomy lot,
God wot,
ink blot.
A happy life with loving wife and cheery tot,
a country cott
in rustic spot
with garden plot
are what
it's not.
No, doom and gloom are what
we've got.
Greasy Joan doth keel the pot,
the snot
-ful tot
whinges a lot.
The garden plot
has black spot,
the country cott
has dry rot
and wet rot.
The upshot
is: our poor poet, the dull clot,
the crackpot,
legs it off at a brisk trot
to become a drunken sot,
and who is there who cares a jot?
Life's not
so hot,
God wot,
poets are a gloomy lot.

# A Painted Ship Inside a Painted Ocean

A little ship sailed with bright flags flying
Through pink and grey seas with the sea birds crying.
Deep she ploughed, her sailors on their knees,
Till she sank to the bottom of the pink grey seas,
And drowned men lay where the fishes play
And seaweed swayed through the clean-picked skulls,
To the mournful cry of the pink grey gulls,
       Down among the dead men.

There were jewelled chalices and chests of gold,
Dead men on the decks and treasure in the hold,
There were knives and cutlasses, muskets and swords,
Sabres and scimitars in pirate hoards,
And wrecked ships lay where the fishes play
And broken nets swayed round the bladderwrack,
For the dead are dead and will never come back,
       Down among the dead men,
      Down among the dead,
       Down among
       Down.

## To His Fast Lover, To Slow Down a Bit

Now we have all the world and time,
To rush at things would be a crime;
Let us sit down and plan our lives,
Pray soon the happy day arrives
We'll get a mortgage, sort things out,
Get into property, look about,
And find ourselves, through river fogs,
A penthouse, in the Isle of Dogs.
Though we may have to wait awhile,
We'll furnish it in lavish style:
Three thousand for that antique chest,
But thirty thousand for the rest.
For Lady, you deserve this state.
Don't hurry on at such a rate.
Please, don't disturb me at my work,
The Chairman mustn't see me shirk.
The merchant bank's a private place,
But none, I think, do there embrace.
Please don't subject me to attacks
And give me back my filofax,
My calculator, mobile phone,
And please, O please, leave me alone.
I can't afford it to be late
Through the iron stockmarket gate,
For at my back I always hear
The futures market, hurrying near.
Don't feel too good, don't feel too bright,
Please, Josephine, please, not tonight.

## Recycled Poems

Old sailor, village bore,
Catches guest at church door.
Leaves him feeling very cross,
Blames that bloody albatross.

Walked a lot, for hours and hours,
Saw some pretty yellow flowers.
Didn't know names of the hills,
But think the flowers were daffodils.

Our pest controller uses a pipe,
He's good, no corpses and no smell
And for a Deutschmark extra,
He'll sort the kids as well.

English villagers are a lovesome lot, God wot,
Though some can be a bit funny.
Why don't you wind that old church clock?
And bugger me, that's the same jar of honey.

Bird sings. Quite good.
Goes further into wood.
Feel depressive, quite excessive.
Knew I should.

"I've been called a lot of things, but never a sacred river,"
Said Alph. "What a funny notion."
"Oh, I don't know," said his friend Fred, "When you've had
A potion, down at the Damsel and Dulcimer,
You don't 'alf meander with a mazy motion."

Sir Lancelot
Felt such a clot,
Singing, "Tirra lirra."
The Lady of Shalott
Cared not a jot.
She was bothered about that mirror.

And an extra verse that Blake should have added —
"Tiger, tiger, hunting food,
May I say that I taste good?
Tiger, tiger, I insist.
I'm a conservationist."

Wish I was back
For the start of the tax year.
I say this, sitting prettily
In Italy.

# What Poets Say of Shepherds

"O envy the shepherd's sweet lot.
From dawn until dusk he doth play."

3am in the lambing shed
And a north east wind straight from the Urals
Is raising the roof. Sheets of corrugated
Iron clash to the beat of the battered shed doors.
Sleet dances round the swaying, naked light bulb.
3am in the lambing shed.

"His flocks are folded, he comes home at night
As merry as a king in his delight."

He is up to the elbow in mucus and blood,
Trying to turn an unborn lamb.
A twist, a tug and then, faintly bleating,
It lies on the bloodied straw,
Its every breath a struggle, it's barely alive.
He takes a wisp to wipe its nose and mouth.
On one side of the lamb's head
There is no eye. Not even a socket.
Then he notices that its forelegs
Do not exist below the joint.
This lamb could have been borne
On the sour winds from the Chernobyl clouds.
Its mother quietly dies.
He takes the lamb by the hind legs
And slams its head against the wall,
Then tosses the small corpse onto the pile of rubbish —
Two more dead lambs, some afterbirths —
Waiting to be burnt.

"The happy shepherds, careless by the fire,
There play their pipes and strum upon the lyre."

3am in the lambing shed.
At dawn he will stumble back
Into the house, have breakfast,
Do the other work of the farm,
Then it's his night for sleep,
Unless the vet student wakes him:
"That ewe'll never make it on her own,
Can I try a Caesar?"

"A happy and carefree life is his,
O lucky shepherd boy whose life is bliss."

## La Belle Ville Sans Transport

"O, what can ail thee, Traveller,
Alone and palely loitering,
When London streets are bleak and bare
    And church bells ring?"

"'Tis Christmastide and that is why
I'm haggard and I'm woebegone,
The buses all have left the streets
    And no trains run.

I hied to London Transport's grot,
Searching for timetables and staff,
But just a cleaner did I see, who said,
    'Don't make me laugh.'

I called a taxi to my house,
I summoned it by telephone.
The driver of it looked at me
    And made sweet moan.

'What, take you out to Cricklewood
On Christmas Day? Ho, no way, Squire.'
He putteth down his little flag.
    'I'm not for hire.'

I cannot walk to Cricklewood
On Christmas Day. It is too far.
And I have supped a mort of ale,
    Can't take the car.

So that is why I loiter here,
With presents I have wrapped with care,
Good cheer that I had hoped to share
With friends who all have gathered there
In Cricklewood; now I despair.
Though all the rest may have a ball,
      La belle ville sans transport
         Hath me in thrall."

## Such Stuff as Dreams

It's a quiet, leafy suburb, peaceful, mainly middle-class,
With well-trimmed privet hedges and close-cut, weedless grass,
Where life seems calm and ordered and nothing's out of place;
Each family is average and smooth and dull each face.

But wait till night has fallen and midnight's chimes ring out:
Strange sounds and sights bemuse the mind of anyone about.
Though no one talks of these by day: don't ask the reason why:
Just watch the wall, my darling, while the payphone thieves
                                         trot by

While the hard hats and the pointy heads join battle in the street
And the garden gnomes dance round their pool and stamp their
                                         little feet,
The drunk nurse meets the naked groom, whose stag night has
                                         turned sour
And Elvis, wearing antlers, swoons over his guitar.

In the empty house, performing fleas are dancing in the bath,
Tap dancing to the music that comes floating up the path
From the company of wolves who serenade the fickle moon,
And a sad, blue ballet dancer shovels peas up with a spoon.

And up the river, silently, the jellyfish float in
On a crime wave, full of mystery, magic, muck and sin.
And up by the allotments, with a short, sharp, savage bark,
The dog who knows his onions goes on digging in the dark.

The biker mourns his late, flat pal and contemplates Nepal,
And the old man dies in the quiet ravine, over the garden wall.
But chaos must be concluded, gaudy, gory nights must end,
And the status quo be preserved, you know, either by foe or
                                         friend.

On the outskirts, the small-holding, masquerading as a farm,
Has a cockerel which crows at dawn, sounding day's alarm.
The insubstantial shadows fade and melt into thin air,
The fleas have ceased their dancing, wolves slink to den
                                                    and lair.

The jelly fish float out again, the dog puts back his spade,
And Teddy bears become, once more, sober, stuffed and staid.
The payphone thieves trot back again, Telecom and go,
The talkative tigers turn for home, grumbling soft and low.

The poor blue dancer's turned quite green, full of frozen peas.
The pestered woman, with a judo kick, brings the pesterer to
                                                    his knees.
The tattooed lady totters off for plastic surgery,
And the night life of the wild, wild town is a fading memory.

## Choices

"That is my ram," thought Abraham.
He stared aghast, from it, caught in the thicket,
To his son, Isaac, bound on the altar of the Lord.

Without that ram
All his new ewes would be barren.
He had bargained long and painfully to win it
From Bethuel of the Perrizites.
It had cost him five good heifers
And the wall-eyed goat
And Sarah's turtle doves.

His new flock.
Farming so difficult.

Surely he would have other sons.
What a choice.
The ram and the boy both pleaded with a fading voice.
Abraham picked up the knife.

"Don't look back,"
Said Lot urgently,
Knowing that was the best way
To make sure she would disobey.
"Don't look back."
But she did. She was leaving so much:
The house, the hens, the tethered goat
And her new geranium cuttings.
And where were the children?
She looked back.

And Lot was quite pleased.
He had a little lady waiting for him in another city.
But O Lot, O horror, she was living in Gomorrah.

## Duet

He loved her, passionato,
For he thought her allegretto.
Her response was moderato
As she thought that he was lento.

She said, "It's not comodo,"
When he asked her sotto voce,
But his approach was quite legato,
She began to think him dolce.

She came to him andante
And then accelerando,
His heart beat presto presto,
Agitato, affretando.

Their affair soon lost its brio
And it was diminuendo,
Quite pleasant, ma non troppo,
The finale was morendo.

For a while they felt dolore,
But, rigoroso speaking,
They both preferred life solo,
A duet they were not seeking.

## Well, What Did You Expect?

One day I walked into a fairy tale,
With woods and winding paths and graceful trees,
I wandered over hill and over dale,
Smelled the sweet flowers, basked in the soft breeze.

And then I came across an elfin pool
Surrounded by marsh marigolds and bog,
And on a little, lily-leafish stool,
There sat a bright green, palpitating frog.

"Kiss me," he croaked, his bulging eyes alight,
"And so restore me to my princely station.
Young virgin, ancient crone, middle-aged fright,
Any female's lips can save the nation."

"I'm sorry," I said, squelching from the bog,
"I have to say I've reached the time long since
When I'm more fascinated by a talking frog,
Have very little interest in a prince."

Calamity! All fairyland went ape.
The frog prince vanished in a clap of smoke,
A puff of thunder shattered the landscape,
The little lily pond shivered and broke.

And then the woods went wild, the wind whirled strong,
Vast spiders swung from trees, I trod on snails
And fought through thorns. Of course the path had gone.
But it was ever thus in fairy tales.

## British Seaside, British Summer

Sitting on the beach at Eyemouth,
Cold the wind and grey the sea,
Watch the jolly British tourists,
Watch the litter, falling free.

See the peach stones, cigarette ends,
Empty packs of crisps and sweets,
Sticky paper, choc-ice paper,
Remnants of half-eaten treats.

Seagulls mew and swoop and quarrel,
Tasty scraps the tourists drop,
Fish and chips and leave the paper,
Empty cans of beer and pop.

See the children bravely paddle,
Turning blue but won't go back,
Pasty, dimpled, all goose-pimpled,
Wave to mum in plastic mac.

Time to leave this peaceful haven,
Sat so long my feet are numb.
Seem attached to Eyemouth sea wall —
Sitting on some chewing gum.

Pick my way back past the dog dirt,
Weave through sounds of Radio One,
Past little nameless bits of plastic,
British seaside. Jolly fun.

# Northern Epiphany

(The stone relief, probably 12th century, of the adoration of the Magi, is one
of the treasures of St. Gregory's church, Kirknewton, Northumberland.
Of interest is the fact that the Magi appear to be wearing kilts.)


They took the high road, though:
"We'll be away now on the low,"
They told King Herod, then rode south, over
The Grampian mountains, where the snow
Balled under the camels' feet
And where the vicious winter wind blew
Sleet through their thin robes.
On clear nights they saw the Northern Lights
Raking the skies in multi-coloured strobes.

At scattered homesteads, they asked for
And were given shelter, and a place by the midden
For the camels. They sat by smoking fires in draughty bothies,
Drinking fierce malt from rough horn cups
That smelled of sheep, and watched
The lads and lassies reel and fling
Half the long night away. And they were given
Warm clothes of the country, and oatmeal with salt,
Which they gave to the camels, who groaned
And spat and seemed to long for home.

And they came to pass through the Borderlands,
Where a great, silver fish leapt before them,
Out of the swollen River Tweed, guiding their feet
To submerged stepping stones,
So that they seemed to walk on water.
(But three pack-camels there got washed away,
The humps are visible to this day, grassy and wooded now,
Where bright gorse blows, above the town of Melrose.)

And they found the babe in a shepherd's hut,
High in the Cheviot hills,
And out of their sporrans they brought gifts:
White heather, haggis, a cairngorm.
But the swaddled bairn lay fast asleep,
Lulled by the bleat of Cheviot sheep.
So they left the lad who was born to be king
And, knowing they would not come back again,
They went home another way, past the land-linked island
That would be Lindisfarne.

They sometimes wondered, as their old men's minds
Grew wandering and dim, where the baby was
And what had happened to him.

# The House Without Windows

I always look for it, along the Jedburgh road.
Every time I pass it, it's been newly painted.
It stands alone, an eyeless, white-washed house.
The lawn is manicured, the fence seems sound.
Someone is keeping up appearances.

Who built this house and ordered all its windows
To be blind? They are black-rimmed lines
Painted on the white-wash.
There is no door.

Is that because there's someone walled inside?
An errant wife, enduring punishment,
Ancient mad mother, mumbling
At the edges of dementia,
Defiant daughter, splitting her nails
On the hard stone, straining to reach her lover?
Is that the muffled, desperate howling
Of a chained, starved dog?

One day I will not pass. I'll stop the car,
Go up the tidy path and, on the freshly
White-washed wall, I'll paint a blood-red door.
And then I'll turn the handle
And go in.

# In the Museum at Aquae Sulis

On a tombstone, carved two thousand years ago,
This inscription names:
> "MERCATILLA
> Slave and freedwoman,
> An orphan, she was fostered by
> MANIUS."

And in his family she was so loved
They knew her age down to the day.

> From slavery to freedom
> From orphan to foster-child
> From birth to death
In "One year, six months, twelve days."

# Black Death

Ancroft Village, May 1348

Abroad in the land is the Angel of Death,
His hand on the people lies heavy and dark,
The beat of his wings and his stinking breath

Stifle the song of the morning lark,
Smother the scent of May blossom and flower,
And the cross on the door is the Black Angel's mark.

The stench of decay is his terrible power;
In the sweet month of May the last villagers die.
No servant of God tolls the bell in the tower,

No room in the plague pit, where too many lie.
They burn down the village, then bury it deep,
Cover corpses and cottages, pile the earth high.

Now clover and meadow-grass grow where the sheep
Safely graze on green hillocks and a sweet bird sings
A Mass for the dead, since there's none left to weep.

It is said, through the soft wind, a church bell rings,
But you hear, in the wild wind, the Black Angel's wings.